THE VACCINATION
DEBATE

THE VACCINATION DEBATE

BY JILL SHERMAN

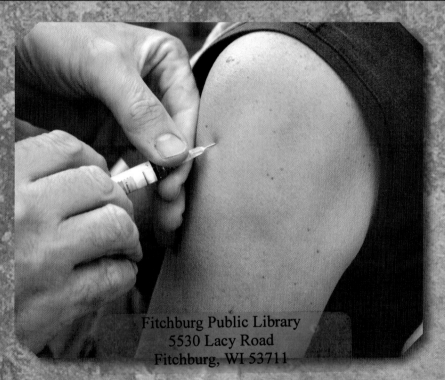

Content Consultant
Alexandra Stewart, JD
Assistant Research Professor, Department of Health Policy
George Washington University Medical Center

ABDO
Publishing Company

CREDITS

Published by ABDO Publishing Company, 8000 West 78th Street, Edina, Minnesota 55439. Copyright © 2011 by Abdo Consulting Group, Inc. International copyrights reserved in all countries. No part of this book may be reproduced in any form without written permission from the publisher. The Essential Library™ is a trademark and logo of ABDO Publishing Company.

Printed in the United States of America,
North Mankato, Minnesota
052010
092010

Editor: Holly Saari
Copy Editor: Sarah Frigon
Interior Design and Production: Kazuko Collins
Cover Design: Kazuko Collins

Library of Congress Cataloging-in-Publication Data
Sherman, Jill.
  The vaccination debate / Jill Sherman.
    p. cm. — (Essential viewpoints)
  Includes bibliographical references and index.
  ISBN 978-1-61613-526-3
  1. Vaccination—Juvenile literature. 2. Vaccination—Public opinion—Juvenile literature. I. Title.
  RA638.S525 2011
  614.4'7—dc22

                        2010002658

TABLE OF CONTENTS

Some Mississippi parents who do not want their children receiving vaccines choose to homeschool them.

VACCINES AND ILLNESS

ebra and Curtis Barnes of Mississippi
are opposed to their state's vaccination
policy. Mississippi requires that students be
vaccinated for a variety of infectious diseases—
hepatitis B, tetanus, whooping cough, polio,

measles, and chicken pox—if they are to enroll in schools or enter day-care centers. Unless children cannot receive these shots because of medical reasons, they must comply. This policy is intended to protect the public's health, because infectious diseases can spread easily in public places such as schools. But some parents who are wary of the dangers associated with vaccination believe that policies mandating the practice infringe on their rights to choose how best to raise their children.

To avoid vaccination, the Barneses chose to homeschool two of their children. Instead of learning in a classroom with a paid teacher, the children are taught at home by one of their parents. Instead of shots, the Barneses help their children maintain healthy lifestyles and strong immune systems. "If you want to vaccinate your children, go ahead. But don't force me to vaccinate my children. These children are entrusted to us," Debra Barnes said.[1]

Mothers' Loss of Faith

Paul Offit, a pediatrician and the chief of infectious diseases at the Children's Hospital of Philadelphia, realizes the skepticism of parents toward vaccinations: "For most mothers, vaccinations become a matter of faith—faith in pharmaceutical companies, faith in public health officials—and I think there's been an erosion of faith."[2]

Vaccines and Religion

Some people refuse to receive vaccinations because of their religious beliefs. For example, religions such as Islam have restrictions against certain vaccines because they are derived from animals. The vaccines would violate the dietary restrictions of these religions.

The Catholic Church opposes abortion, which is the expulsion of an embryo or a fetus. Some vaccines are made from stem cells taken from discarded embryos. However, Catholic tradition holds that people who receive these types of vaccinations are not cooperating with abortion, especially if no other vaccine is available.

As president of the Jackson chapter of the Mississippi Vaccination Information Center, Barnes is working to change Mississippi's policy. She hopes that new laws will allow parents more freedom in choosing whether to vaccinate their children, because the Barneses are not alone in their decision. In most states, parents can receive permission to waive shots based on their personal beliefs. This is called opting out. Mississippi and West Virginia are the only two states that prohibit parents from opting out of vaccinations for philosophical or religious reasons.

A growing number of parents are choosing against vaccination for fear of its potential side effects. Though all states require shots for school-age children, parents are seeking exemptions from this requirement. In Massachusetts, the number of parents of kindergarteners seeking exemptions more than doubled

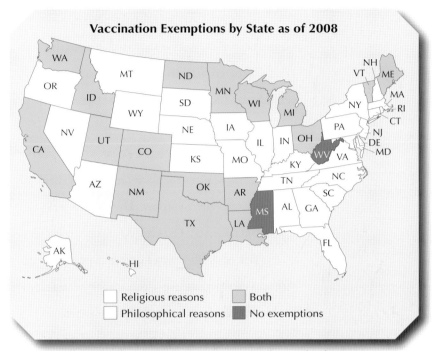

Vaccination Exemptions by State as of 2008

Legend:
- Religious reasons
- Philosophical reasons
- Both
- No exemptions

All states allow vaccination exemptions for medical reasons. All states but West Virginia and Mississippi allow exemptions for philosophical or religious reasons.

between 1996 and 2006—from 210 in 1996 to 474 in 2006. The number of exemptions represents only 0.6 percent of kindergarteners in Massachusetts, but the trend has many health officials concerned.

INFECTIOUS DISEASES

Infectious diseases were once a serious threat to a person's health. But, in the twentieth century, the development of vaccines and an increased focus on hygiene stamped out many of these threats to the public's health. Instances of measles, diphtheria, whooping cough, rabies, tetanus, and polio decreased dramatically, which led to a sharp increase in average life expectancy.

Most health experts credit vaccination for this phenomenon. Vaccination is considered one of the most important advancements in the history of medicine. Medical professionals worry that if people follow the Barneses' example and stop vaccinating their children, public health may suffer.

Nonvaccination could allow disease to spread. Many dangerous diseases that were once prevented through vaccines may flare up again. And public health officials would be poorly equipped to treat a major outbreak of measles, tetanus, or whooping cough today. After not having treated the diseases on a large

Negative Reactions

The federal Vaccine Adverse Event Reporting System receives approximately 30,000 reports a year about negative side effects of immunizations. About 3,000 to 4,500 of these reports are classified as serious. Serious reactions include allergic reactions, long-term seizures, coma, and brain damage.

scale for several generations, the medical community has not stockpiled enough treatment to deal with a large outbreak.

Opposition to Vaccines

Despite vaccines' positive results, they can have negative side effects. Sore arms, fevers, and rashes may result from some vaccines, as may rarer but more serious side effects such as convulsions and nerve and brain damage—and even death.

A typical vaccine contains a weakened sample of the illness it protects against. In most cases, the vaccine helps a person's immune system develop antibodies to fight off future infection. But in rare instances, a person may develop the infection present in the vaccine.

Furthermore, vaccinations are not 100 percent effective, and they can wear off. In rare cases, people who are vaccinated will not be protected. Opponents of vaccines contend that a strong, healthy immune system should be able to produce antibodies that fight off infections; a healthy body can develop lifelong immunity to each strain of illness it resists.

The most troubling issue for many parents regarding vaccines is the treatment's potential link to autism. Autism is a serious medical disorder that develops in children. It severely impairs their ability to socialize and communicate. A number of parents of autistic children have reported that their children were developing normally until they were vaccinated. This potential link has given some parents pause when they are deciding whether to vaccinate their children. Medical researchers do not know what causes autism, and no known cure exists.

In Favor of Vaccines

Proponents of vaccines point out that no medical procedure is without risk—including vaccination. But they say the benefits far outweigh the drawbacks: vaccines have saved millions of lives and prevented untold amounts of pain and suffering. Each year, vaccines are credited with preventing approximately 14 million infections.

According to the Institute of Medicine, "Immunization is widely regarded as one of the most effective and beneficial tools for protecting

A Parent's Opinion

Evelyn Gonzalez of Boston, Massachusetts, believes in the effectiveness of vaccines. She writes, "I've certainly had my concerns about inoculations. However, I'm even more concerned about parents sending children to public places and schools knowing how easily disease is spread, when they haven't been given their vaccines."[3]

the public's health."[4] Not vaccinating puts the public's health at risk. Those who go unvaccinated by choice increase the risk of developing an illness and passing it on to others who are too young or chronically ill and cannot be fully vaccinated.

Already, outbreaks of measles and other diseases preventable by vaccination are increasing. In 2008, the Centers for Disease Control and Prevention (CDC) reported that 64 measles cases had occurred between January and April of that year—the most that had occurred in that span of time since 2001. Of the 64 cases, 63 people were unvaccinated or had unknown vaccination status.

Dr. Anne Schuchat, director of the National Center

Vaccine Schedule for Children

The CDC's Advisory Committee on Immunization Practices (ACIP) advises that all children receive a variety of immunizations. As of 2010, the schedule for children from birth to age six included vaccines for:

- hepatitis B
- rotavirus
- diphtheria, tetanus, pertussis (whooping cough)
- *haemophilus influenzae* Type B
- pneumococcal
- inactivated poliovirus
- influenza
- measles, mumps, rubella
- varicella (chicken pox)
- meningococcal (meningitis)
- hepatitis A

By following the recommended vaccine schedule, children could receive more than 25 shots by the time they are 18 years old.

for Immunization and Respiratory Diseases at the CDC said, "We are seeing more outbreaks that look different, concentrated among intentionally unimmunized people. I hope they are not the beginning of a worse trend."[5]

Medical professionals worry that parents who decide against shots do not understand how serious illnesses such as whooping cough and measles are. Healthy immune systems are not enough to prevent these illnesses. Many parents today have never witnessed the horrors of vaccine-preventable infectious diseases. If they had, they might be more willing to vaccinate. Mark Sawyer, an infectious disease specialist and pediatrician at Rady Children's Hospital in San Diego, commented,

> *The very success of immunizations has turned out to be an Achilles' heel. Most of these parents have never seen measles, and don't realize it could be a bad disease so they turn their concerns to unfounded risks. They do not perceive risk of the disease but perceive risk of the vaccine.*[6]

In addition, the medical community is critical of the supposed link between vaccines and autism. Autism often begins to show at the age when children are routinely vaccinated. Researchers say that the link is coincidental, that no scientific evidence proves a connection.

The Heart of the Controversy

Many arguments can be made for and against vaccination, and the decision to vaccinate can be complex. The threat of a child developing illnesses such as measles, tetanus, and whooping cough has decreased significantly. As a result, parents have become more skeptical of vaccines and are less willing to put up with their side effects. But the medical community believes that this viewpoint is shortsighted. Infectious diseases can spread rapidly. Already measles cases are on the rise as a result of more parents opting out of shots for their children. People who are not vaccinated put their own health and public health at risk.

Many dispute the risks. Is the bigger threat to society a highly contagious outbreak or the side

"When I vaccinate my child against tetanus, which grows in the soil, shelters in rusty nails, and does not spread from child to child, I am protecting my child alone. But I also vaccinate her against measles, polio, whooping cough, chickenpox, mumps, meningitis, hepatitis, diphtheria, and pneumonia. In doing so I help eliminate the safe haven from which these organisms might launch an attack on somebody else's child, on a teenager whose immunity has waned, or on an adult who was never vaccinated. Public health means recognizing that complete personal responsibility is unattainable. Within limits, we must all help look after one another—that is our social contract."[7]

—*Arthur Allen,* Vaccine: The Controversial Story of Medicine's Greatest Lifesaver effects of a widely used vaccine? Individual rights are another issue. Should an individual have the right to make a personal choice that might put others at risk? ⌐

Ann Schuchat, director of the National Center for Immunization and Respiratory Diseases at the CDC, is a proponent of vaccination.

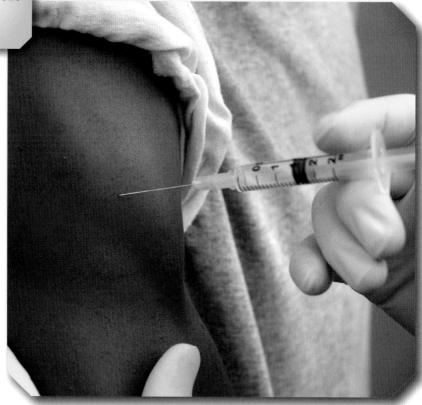

A doctor gives a patient a vaccine shot.

WHAT IS VACCINATION?

Vaccination is the process of making someone immune to an infection or disease. Vaccines contain killed or modified microorganisms—either viruses or bacteria—that will trigger an immune system response.

The immune system is made up of the thymus, spleen, lymph nodes, cells, and antibodies. It protects the body against harmful organisms or other damaging substances that enter the body. Organisms that cause disease are called pathogens. They include viruses, bacteria, and other disease-causing microbes.

A healthy immune system is easily able to recognize pathogens. It produces antibodies that fight off a particular infection. Once an infection has been resisted, those antibodies stay in the body. They provide immunity to that infection. If the pathogens return, the immune system will release the antibodies more quickly than it did the first time. The person will probably not even know he or she had the infection.

Vaccines use the body's immune system. A typical vaccine contains a weakened version of a pathogen. Sometimes the pathogen has been altered so that it cannot cause illness. When the pathogen enters the body, the immune system creates antibodies to combat it. In most cases, the weakened pathogen does not make the person sick. In the future, when the person comes in contact with the real pathogen, the immune system will be able to respond rapidly to create more antibodies to fight off infection. Most likely, the person will not get sick.

A Vaccine's Components

In addition to the virus or bacteria, vaccines contain several substances, including suspending fluid, preservatives, and adjuvants. The suspending fluid does not have any medicinal qualities. It supplies the liquid base of the shot and is usually water or saline (a solution of salt and water). However, some suspending fluids may contain calf serum, chicken egg protein, or gelatin made from pig parts. Influenza vaccines, which contain egg protein, have caused reactions in children with allergies to eggs. People who do not eat beef or pork because of religious reasons usually can receive vaccines that do not contain calf serum or gelatin.

Vaccines also contain preservatives, which allow them to be stored until they are needed. A once-common preservative, thimerosal, contains trace amounts of mercury. Though the amount of mercury has not been known to

Food and Drug Administration

Today, all vaccines have to be approved by the Food and Drug Administration (FDA). The FDA ensures that all vaccines in the United States are as safe and effective as current scientific knowledge will allow.

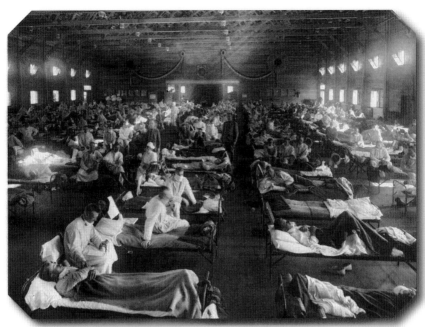

Prior to the development of vaccines, contagious diseases often reached pandemic levels.

cause poisoning, some parents have been concerned about thimerosal's effects in young children. The preservative is no longer used in most vaccines for children, and if requested, patients can receive a thimerosal-free influenza vaccine.

Adjuvants are substances that are added to vaccines to intensify the immune system response. As of 2010, the only one allowed for use was alum. Alum may cause inflammation at the injection site, but other side effects are rare.

TYPES OF VACCINES

Several kinds of vaccines exist. Some contain live viruses or live bacteria from an infectious disease. These viruses or bacteria have been rendered harmless in a laboratory, though they resemble their original forms very closely. This type of vaccine is used for measles and smallpox vaccination.

Other vaccines contain viruses or bacteria that have been killed and so cannot cause disease when injected. However, the structure of the virus or bacteria can still trigger the immune system to respond. Such vaccines are more likely to cause an allergic reaction. They also often require booster shots, or additional doses administered later on. This type of vaccine is used for typhoid vaccination.

A purified vaccine uses a portion of the disease-causing agent or one of its chemical components—only

Vaccine-preventable Diseases

As of 2010, vaccines could prevent anthrax, cervical cancer, diphtheria, hepatitis A, hepatitis B, Haemophilus influenzae type b, HPV (human papillomavirus), influenza, Japanese encephalitis, measles, meningitis, monkeypox, mumps, pertussis (whooping cough), pneumococcal, polio, rabies, rotavirus, rubella, shingles, smallpox, tetanus, typhoid, tuberculosis, varicella, and yellow fever. However, not all vaccines are 100 percent effective, such as that of typhoid.

the element that causes an immune system response. The part of the virus or bacteria that triggers disease is removed. This type of vaccine is used for some whooping cough vaccination.

Some vaccines are made from toxins secreted by bacteria. The toxins are made inactive in a laboratory. They are no longer harmful but still provide protection against the actual bacteria that cause the illness. This type of vaccine is used for tetanus and diphtheria vaccination.

Vaccination Works

Doctors and health officials often point to vaccination's proven track record. Prior to the polio vaccine, 13,000 to 20,000 cases of paralyzing polio occurred

Top Ten Public Health Achievements

During the twentieth century, great strides were made in improving public health. According to the CDC, the most notable advancements in the United States include:

- Vaccination
- Motor-vehicle safety
- Safer workplaces
- Control of infectious diseases
- Decline in deaths from coronary heart disease and stroke
- Safer and healthier foods
- Healthier mothers and babies
- Family planning
- Fluoridation of drinking water
- Recognition of tobacco use as a health hazard[1]

These achievements have greatly increased the overall health and life expectancy of U.S. residents.

every year in the United States. Approximately 48,000 cases of smallpox occurred annually in the United States before the smallpox vaccine was developed. In 1921—prior to the diphtheria vaccine— approximately 200,000 cases of the disease were reported in the United States, with approximately 15,000 resulting in death. Since 2000, no cases of polio have been reported, and only five cases of diphtheria have occurred in the United States. Doctors credit vaccination with the remarkable drop in these illnesses.

Other vaccine-preventable illnesses, including measles, meningitis, and tetanus, have seen a sharp decline as well. According to David Keller, former chief of the Infectious Disease and Epidemiology Program with the New Mexico Department of Health,

> *Data from many studies lead the overwhelming majority of public health experts to the conclusion that the use of vaccines has prevented—and will continue to prevent—tens of thousands of deaths and millions of episodes of diseases in children in the U.S. alone.*[2]

CDC director Julie Gerberding spoke about influenza vaccination in 2003.

A hospital in Asia housed many patients with smallpox in 1962.

THE RISE OF VACCINATION

*I*n the United States, vaccination became widespread around the mid-nineteenth century when vaccines for measles, mumps, rubella, whooping cough, and tetanus became part of a child's standard medical treatment. But the history of vaccination goes back hundreds of years. The first vaccine ever created—in 1796—was for smallpox, a disease that no longer exists. The history of the smallpox shows how vaccination eliminated one of the world's most deadly diseases.

A Devastating Disease

Smallpox was once the most dangerous disease to affect humans. It probably arose in Africa, possibly as early as 10,000 BCE. From there, it spread to India and throughout Asia and Europe. Later, it traveled to the Americas with European colonists.

Smallpox devastated entire populations, killing about one-third of those who became infected. During some epidemics, the mortality rate reached 80 percent. In the twentieth century alone, smallpox is estimated to have killed approximately 300 million people worldwide.

Outbreaks, Epidemics, and Pandemics

Several terms are used to describe the severity of a spreading disease. When a large number of people in an area contract a particular illness, an *outbreak* has occurred. Public health officials are alerted, and they try to find the cause of the outbreak so that it can be controlled. Area doctors are also alerted so they can better treat their patients.

When an illness spreads rapidly and affects a large number of people, it is considered an *epidemic*. Epidemics are more widespread and affect a much greater number of people than do outbreaks. If an epidemic is limited to a particular geographic area, it is considered an endemic disease. But because of globalization, people and goods travel across the world every day. Diseases are less likely to be limited to one area. When an illness spreads throughout the world, it is called a *pandemic*.

A child in India with smallpox in 1974

Smallpox began with a high fever. After two to
four days, infected people developed sores on their
hands and feet. The sores then spread, covering their
bodies and faces. The sores grew larger, becoming
painful and filling with puss. Other symptoms
included headache, vomiting, confusion, and coma.
Those who did not die were often left badly scarred
or blinded from the disease.

In the late nineteenth century, English historian
Thomas Macaulay wrote, "Smallpox was always
present, filling the churchyard with corpses,

tormenting with constant fear all whom it had not yet stricken, leaving on those whose lives it spared the hideous traces of its power."[1]

EARLY IMMUNIZATIONS

For centuries, people watched helplessly as their loved ones suffered through smallpox infections. But they knew that any person who survived the disease was safe from further infection. This knowledge prompted tenth-century Chinese healers to try to induce mild cases of smallpox in healthy people to avoid a more dangerous infection. The healers would blow some dried matter from the smallpox pustules into a healthy person's nostrils. This practice of inducing mild cases of smallpox to prevent more severe infections is now called variolation. It was one of the earliest attempts to bring about immunity.

Variolation was successful at inducing immunity. However, it did have risks. People who underwent the procedure all became sick with smallpox. Usually the cases were mild, but sometimes serious illness developed. Variolation had a 2 to 3 percent death rate, but many people were encouraged by its success. By the sixteenth century, the practice spread to Europe and then to the Americas. In Europe, children who underwent variolation were confined to special hospitals where they were cared for until free of any signs of the illness.

EDWARD JENNER AND THE SMALLPOX VACCINE

In England in the mid-eighteenth century, eight-year-old Edward Jenner was among the many children who underwent variolation. At age 13, Jenner became an apprentice to Daniel Ludlow, a local surgeon, in order to train to become a doctor. During his apprenticeship, Jenner first learned of a connection between smallpox and the less common cowpox.

Jenner met a young milkmaid who had never undergone variolation. He was surprised when the girl told him, "I shall never have smallpox for I have had cowpox. I shall never have an ugly pockmarked face."[2] Cowpox was an uncommon illness, but its symptoms were much milder than smallpox's.

Variolation Comes to England

Lady Mary Wortley Montague introduced variolation to England in 1721. Her husband was ambassador to Turkey, and she learned of the practice while in Constantinople. She was so impressed by the process that she had both of her children variolated. She convinced the Princess of Wales to do the same with her children. Variolation soon became popular in England, and the number of children who became sick with smallpox was greatly reduced.

Jenner left the countryside to continue his studies, but he remained fascinated by the milkmaid's claim. Though it had provided him immunity from smallpox, Jenner's own variolation had been a miserable experience. He was intrigued by the possibility that cowpox might be a way for others to avoid such hardship.

Cowpox was uncommon, and few had written about it. To research the disease, Jenner asked questions of nearly every doctor or farmer he met. Jenner observed that farm people who had previously

Jonas Salk and the Polio Vaccine

Polio is a serious viral infection that was common in the early twentieth century. Polio often affected children, causing fever, headache, drowsiness, sore throat, and vomiting. Many of those infected with polio experienced mild symptoms or even no symptoms at all. However, polio could leave the infected person paralyzed for life.

Jonas Salk was a U.S. scientist who studied disease and preventative medicine. During the 1950s, Salk developed a vaccine for polio. The vaccine was an injection containing the three types of the virus that were known at that time. Salk inoculated himself, his wife, and his three sons. In April 1955, the vaccine was declared to be safe and effective, and it was licensed for use in the United States. The Salk vaccine greatly reduced the number of polio infections in the years following.

In 1961, a competing vaccine was licensed for use in the United States. It had the advantage of being administered orally and not requiring booster shots. The oral vaccine became preferred over Salk's until it was discovered it caused a small number of people to become infected with polio. Afterward, Salk's vaccine again became the preferred one.

contracted cowpox never developed smallpox symptoms. In 1796, Jenner variolated a young boy using cowpox pathogens. After the boy recovered from cowpox, Jenner variolated him with smallpox. The boy did not become sick.

Soon after this experiment, Jenner published a paper recommending the practice he called *vaccination,* which stems from the Latin word for cow, *vacca.* Jenner's smallpox vaccine took off. By 1801, more than 100,000 people had received it. Henry Cline, a surgeon in London, England, wrote Jenner, "I think substituting cow-pox poison for the smallpox promises to be one of the greatest improvements that has ever been made in medicine."[3]

Jenner's smallpox vaccine was gradually improved and used to inoculate millions of people. It was so successful, in fact, that in 1980, the World Health Organization (WHO) declared smallpox to have been eradicated.

World Health Organization

The World Health Organization (WHO), founded in 1948, is an organization that operates under the United Nations. It works to create better health care throughout the world. WHO works toward disease prevention through immunization programs as well as by improving the quality of drinking water and creating better sewage disposal. It monitors health trends in order to better protect people from infectious disease. WHO is also a leader in health research and establishing standard health practices.

Edward Jenner developed the process of vaccination in the late eighteenth century.

In 1800, a contaminated smallpox vaccine infected many Massachusetts residents, some of whom died.

A History of
Vaccine Errors

Despite the success of the smallpox vaccine, there is another side to the history of vaccination. Beginning with smallpox, vaccine errors have led to outbreaks and even death. Examples from history show the ways that vaccines can cause illness.

A Smallpox Outbreak

In the late eighteenth century and early nineteenth century, the science of studying disease was still very new. No method existed to identify pathogens. Consequently, Edward Jenner did not always know the contents of his vaccines. The only way he knew whether they contained cowpox or weakened smallpox was by how a patient reacted to a vaccine—when it was too late to change anything.

In 1800, Jenner sent his vaccine to Marblehead, Massachusetts, but the vaccine was contaminated. Within a month, the town became the site of a smallpox outbreak. Approximately 1,000 people became ill with smallpox and 68 people died.

Disaster in Lübeck

More than 100 years later, another outbreak occurred across the Atlantic Ocean. Tuberculosis had been a problem in Lübeck, Germany, for a long time. So when a tuberculosis vaccine became available, public health officials brought the vaccine to the city. In 1929, the vaccine was given to 242 children. A great number of them developed acute tuberculosis. The children experienced severe symptoms including diarrhea, fever, nausea, and projectile vomiting. Later, the glands in their necks became very swollen, blocking their airways.

Within a few weeks, 72 children had died. Many who survived were left with brain damage and other complications. An investigation revealed that two lab directors had mistakenly contaminated the vaccine, leading to the epidemic.

Dangerous Diphtheria Vaccines

Diphtheria is a severe respiratory disease that causes sore throat, fever, breathing difficulties, temporary paralysis, and possible death. Early diphtheria vaccines contained a mixture of diphtheria toxin, which is produced by the disease's pathogens, and antitoxin. An antitoxin is meant to counteract the toxin, making it safe for injection. The amounts of toxin and antitoxin in the vaccine had to be just right, or it would make a person ill.

Vaccine Side Effects

With almost all vaccines, there is a risk of pain, redness, or swelling at the injection site. Other, more serious side effects can occur as well. For example, in rare cases the whooping cough vaccine can cause persistent crying or high fever.

Individuals with allergies may risk going into anaphylactic shock because of vaccines. This occurs rarely, because people who receive vaccines are asked about possible allergies beforehand. If a person does go into shock, however, symptoms could include difficulty breathing, abdominal pain, and cramping. If not treated, a person could die—anaphylactic shock is fatal in up to 1 percent of people who experience it.

Scientists developed diphtheria vaccine in a laboratory in the late nineteenth century. In the early twentieth century, a batch of diphtheria vaccine caused many people to become ill with the disease.

In 1919, more than 300 children were vaccinated in Dallas, Texas. But instead of receiving protection from diphtheria, 120 children contracted the disease. The diphtheria toxin had not been completely neutralized, and ten children died. A similar outbreak occurred in Kyoto, Japan, in 1948, when more than 15,000 children were vaccinated with a toxic vaccine. More than 600 children became ill, and 68 died.

During the early twentieth century, diphtheria was a common childhood illness in Queensland, Australia, and many families lost children to the disease. On January 12, 1928, the vaccine was administered to 21 children. Within hours, the children became violently ill. Twelve eventually died. In this case, they did not die from diphtheria. The vaccine had somehow been contaminated with another kind of bacteria.

PROBLEMS WITH POLIO VACCINES

On April 25, 1955, just a few weeks after Jonas Salk's polio vaccine had been released for general use in the United States, an infant was admitted to a Chicago hospital. The child, who had received the polio vaccine just nine days prior, was suffering from paralysis. Several more cases emerged in California. The common

Deadly Side Effects

When seven-month-old Nathan Silvermintz returned from the pediatrician's office after a regular exam in 1991, he began crying steadily. Nathan's mother was told that this was a normal reaction to the diphtheria, pertussis, and tetanus (DPT) shot he had received.

But Nathan's condition worsened. His mother finally called 911 for help. By the time the paramedics arrived, Nathan had collapsed. They worked on him for 45 minutes, but it was no use. The child died.

Afterward, Nathan's parents learned that their son's high-pitched, persistent cries, fever, and collapse were rare side effects of the DPT vaccine. Nathan's parents were awarded compensation for his death. Nine other children who were vaccinated with the same batch of DPT vaccine died.

Stories like these are harsh reminders for some parents that vaccines are not always safe—even today.

factor was the manufacturer of the vaccine: Cutter Laboratories.

On April 27, the Cutter vaccine was recalled. However, a little more than a week later, close friends and family members of the individuals affected by the vaccine began to become sick with polio. The Cutter vaccine contained live, active polio. The virus had mistakenly not been made inactive during the manufacturing process. The Cutter vaccine caused 164 cases of paralysis and ten deaths. In response, the manufacturing process was refined, and the vaccine was made safer.

Then, in the 1960s, another problem with Salk's polio vaccine emerged. The vaccine was prepared using rhesus monkey kidneys, which were often infected with a live virus called SV40. It did not cause disease in the monkeys. However, it was found to have an effect on humans.

This troubling discovery began in 1960, when Dr. Bernice Eddy's research showed that monkey kidney cells could cause cancer in hamsters. However, when Eddy shared her findings with her superiors at the National Institutes of Health, they were dismissed. She was also prevented from publishing her findings, though she presented them without approval at a meeting of the American Cancer Society.

Other researchers identified SV40 as the cancer-causing agent, and they wrote about their findings. As one author wrote, "The measures designed to protect the world from polio may, in their turn, for all we know, lead to some other quite unexpected consequence which may be to man's disadvantage."[1]

People dispute whether these words have proven true. The virus is present in approximately 23 percent of the U.S. population. Also, the CDC acknowledges the link between cancer and SV40, which has been found in several human cancers such as those of the brain, lung, and bones. However, CDC officials do not believe that the prevalence of SV40 is due to polio vaccination. SV40 is present in many children who are too young to have received the shot. Vaccine opponents counter

National Vaccine Information Center

Established in 1982, the National Vaccine Information Center (NVIC) is a private organization that provides information on the potential dangers associated with various vaccines. The center advocates vaccine safety and the rights of parents to make informed decisions about vaccination. The NVIC monitors vaccine development, research, policies, and legislation. It also provides assistance to individuals who believe that they have been harmed by receiving shots.

that the initial vaccines likely introduce the virus, which is then transmitted from person to person. Any damage from the vaccine has already been done.

ATYPICAL MEASLES

In 1963, both a live measles vaccine and a killed measles vaccine were released. The killed vaccine—which had less risk of a child becoming ill with mild measles than with the live vaccine—was widely used in Canada and the United States. However, 54 children who were vaccinated with the killed virus vaccine eventually contracted measles. The antibodies that the vaccine helped develop disappeared too quickly, within about one year. Even with booster shots, the vaccine was ineffective.

Furthermore, children who received these shots were prone to developing a new strain of measles, called atypical measles. Symptoms included headache, muscle pain, pneumonia, and rash. Many children with atypical measles were hospitalized, but they all recovered. Researchers suspect that the killed measles vaccine sensitized children to the measles virus. When they encountered the virus, the children contracted the new strain. The killed measles vaccine was recalled, and atypical measles disappeared with it.

Immunization Action Coalition

The Immunization Action Coalition (IAC) was launched in 1994 in order to increase immunization rates and prevent the spread of illness. The coalition distributes educational information about the need for vaccination. It maintains that vaccines are safe, especially when compared with the complications that result from the spread of vaccine-preventable diseases.

These instances show that vaccines present possible dangers and consequences. More than likely, outbreaks based on faulty vaccines will continue in the future. In the eyes of opponents, the risks of vaccines outweigh the benefits. In particular, they point to what many believe is vaccination's greatest danger: autism.

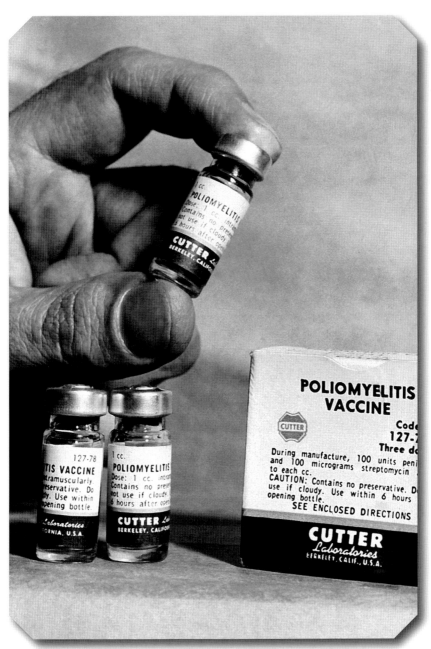

In 1955, the polio vaccine from Cutter Laboratories caused several vaccine recipients to contract polio.

Hannah Poling and her parents at a press conference in 2008

AUTISM AND VACCINES

annah Poling had an uneventful birth, and, according to her parents, she was developing normally. Hannah was a happy, smiling, and engaged child. But in July 2000, when Hannah was 19 months old, her parents took her to the doctor for routine vaccinations. The next day, Hannah developed a high fever, cried, and refused to walk. Three months later, she began showing signs of autism. Hannah would spin herself around and stare at lights and fans. She became socially withdrawn and, for a while, she would not speak.

Hannah's parents, Jon and Terry Poling, blame Hannah's autism on vaccines. "Something happened after the vaccines. She just deteriorated and never came back," said Terry Poling, Hannah's mother.[1]

What happened to Hannah is not unique. Children who develop autism usually show signs of the disease before they are three years old. Often, parents begin to notice the early signs of autism shortly after their child has been vaccinated. For this reason, some parents believe autism is caused by vaccination.

The CDC estimates that autism affects one in every 150 children. As doctors are becoming more knowledgeable about the disorder,

What Is Autism?

Autism is a developmental disorder that impairs a child's social behavior and ability to communicate. Children with autism often show repetitive behavior, such as repeating certain sounds, rocking their bodies, or arranging objects in a particular way. Signs of autism show before a child is three years old.

Children with autism often require special education programs and behavior therapy. With treatment, they may be able to function in society and gain independence. In some cases, early intervention and intensive therapy have reduced or eliminated signs of the disorder.

more children are being diagnosed. The exact cause and nature of autism remain elusive to scientists and researchers. Since no cause is known, some parents believe vaccines may be a contributing factor to the development of the disease. They are reluctant to vaccinate their children if there is even a remote possibility that doing so could cause their children to become autistic.

Hannah Poling's Court Case

In March 2008, a special court ruled that vaccines had negatively affected Hannah Poling. Poling suffers from a mitochondrial disorder, which affects cell metabolism. In addition, Poling had fallen behind on her vaccine schedule. She received a large number of vaccinations in 2000, some containing thimerosal, in order to catch up on required vaccinations. Because of these unusual circumstances, Poling was awarded compensation. But her case would not serve as a precedent in other cases regarding vaccines and autism.

THE WAKEFIELD STUDY

In 1998, British scientist Andrew Wakefield and several of his colleagues published a study that suggested vaccines were directly linked to autism. According to the study, the MMR (measles, mumps, and rubella) vaccine caused inflammation in the intestines. The upset intestines then let toxins into the bloodstream, which could then travel to the brain. The presence of these toxins in the brain, according to the study, could cause autism. After the study was released, fears that vaccines were responsible for autism

Andrew Wakefield attended a hearing to determine if he had acted unethically and unprofessionally throughout his study linking autism and vaccination.

increased. Vaccination rates dropped in Britain and other European countries as well as the United States.

Although the Wakefield study prompted concerns regarding vaccine safety, the reliability of the study has since been called into question. The study was not completed according to accepted scientific procedures. For example, only 12 children were

Advocate for Those with Autism

Actor Jenny McCarthy is an autism advocate. Her son, Evan, was diagnosed with autism. In an open letter to CNN regarding vaccines and autism, McCarthy and another advocate wrote,

"We believe autism is an environmental illness. Vaccines are not the only environmental trigger, but we do think they play a major role. If we are going to solve this problem and finally start to reverse the rate of autism, we need to consider changing the vaccine schedule, reducing the number of shots given and removing certain ingredients that could be toxic to some children.

"We take into account that some children have reactions to medicines like penicillin, for example, yet when it comes to vaccines we are operating as if our kids have a universal tolerance for them. We are acting like ONE SIZE FITS ALL. That is, at the very least, a huge improbability."[2]

studied. Critics contend that only a much larger sample group could begin to yield accurate results. Also, instead of using records, the study relied on parents to remember when their child began to show signs of autism, which had occurred eight years prior to the study.

In addition, an investigation revealed that Wakefield had been paid to conduct the study by lawyers for parents who already believed their children had been harmed by vaccinations. This raised questions about Wakefield's motives and objectivity, and several of the scientists involved in the study retracted its findings in response. In 2010, after a lengthy investigation, a British medical panel stated Wakefield acted unethically. Following this, the medical journal that published the study retracted Wakefield's paper. Wakefield, however, maintains that the study's findings are valid.

Actor Jenny McCarthy at a rally that proposed
the elimination of toxins from vaccines

SCIENTIFIC STUDIES

Since the vaccine-autism controversy first
arose, a great number of studies have looked for
a possible connection. However, as of 2010, no
scientific proof connected vaccines to autism. For
example, a 2002 study in Denmark surveyed more
than 500,000 children and found no statistically

significant link between vaccination and autism. Further studies performed by the CDC, European Union, and private researchers have confirmed that vaccines do not cause autism.

Mercury in Vaccines

Certain chemicals in vaccines have come into question. For example, thimerosal was a common preservative used to prevent vaccines from becoming contaminated with bacteria. The preservative contains trace amounts of mercury. Parents began questioning if the mercury in vaccines led to autism. Though the amount of mercury in vaccines was very small, children were receiving more vaccines than they had been the previous decade.

As a precaution, the U.S. government ordered that thimerosal be removed from or reduced in vaccines for children under the age of six. As a result, the influenza vaccine is the only vaccine for children that contains thimerosal, though a version of the vaccine without the preservative is available upon request. After the removal of thimerosal from most vaccines, there should have been a drop in autism cases if the chemical caused the development of the disease. However, no such decrease occurred.

Vaccines in Court

Many parents who believe that vaccines are responsible for their children's autism have filed claims with the National Vaccine Injury Compensation Program (VICP), which awards compensation for vaccine-related health problems. Between 1999 and 2007, 5,000 autism-related claims were filed with the federal program.

In 2007, a special court began to hear cases involving the link between vaccines and autism. The claims of three families, the Cedillos, the Hazelhursts, and the Snyders, were used as test cases to represent the larger group. The decisions in their

Autism Diagnoses Rise

Scientists acknowledge that more children are being diagnosed with autism than before. However, scientific research has found no link between autism and vaccinations, and, in fact, most scientists doubt that autism can be rooted to one cause. Rather, autism is likely due to a combination of genetic and environmental factors. Babies are more likely to develop autism if they are born with small heads and experience a short period of head growth within their first year. Pregnant women who are exposed to rubella or certain drugs have children who have a higher chance of developing autism.

The increase in autism diagnoses could be a result of doctors having a better understanding of the disorder. Children who once might have been diagnosed as mentally retarded or learning disabled are now diagnosed with autism. In other words, more children are being diagnosed correctly with autism. In addition, related disorders, such as Asperger's syndrome, are sometimes classified as autism.

National Vaccine Injury Compensation Program

Congress created the VICP in 1988. The program is meant to encourage parents to bring their children for shots by providing compensation in the rare cases where injury is caused by vaccination. The program covers all vaccines that are recommended for administration to the public. Since its inception, it has paid $1.18 billion dollars to 1,500 individuals who were harmed by vaccines.

cases would influence the outcomes of similar claims.

In February 2009, after carefully reviewing thousands of pages of scientific evidence and testimony of qualified experts, the judges, called special masters, ruled that no evidence proved childhood vaccinations could cause autism. In the official ruling, one special master wrote,

> After considering the record as a whole, I hold that petitioners have failed to establish . . . that Colten's [an autistic child] condition was caused or significantly aggravated by a vaccine or any component thereof. . . . After careful consideration of all of the evidence, it was abundantly clear that petitioners' theories of causation were speculative and unpersuasive.[3]

The ruling disappointed many people in the autism community, who remain convinced that vaccinations are related to autism. Advocacy groups, such as Autism Speaks, continue to support research to find the cause of autism. ⌐

In 2009, a special court ruled that there was not enough evidence to support the claim that vaccines cause autism.

In 2008, New Jersey parents held a rally to oppose the requirement that children receive influenza vaccinations in order to attend day care.

Opposition to Mandatory Vaccinations

If vaccination were a personal choice with no consequence to society, perhaps no debate would exist. Those who believe in vaccination's link to autism would be free to avoid the medical practice. However, this is not the case.

Mandatory vaccination policies bring the dispute about vaccination's benefits and risks into the area of public debate.

All states require students to be vaccinated against several infectious diseases before entering school, but not all vaccines are mandatory. For public and private school admittance, state governments have made mandatory vaccines for illnesses that are the most severe threat to public health, such as measles and polio. Government officials believe such policy protects the public from outbreaks of infectious diseases that happen more easily in public places such as schools. However, every state allows parents to opt out of mandatory vaccinations for medical reasons, and several states allow opt outs for religious or philosophical reasons. Some parents who reside in states that do not allow religious or philosophical opt outs oppose mandatory vaccination. They do not believe the government should be allowed to require medical procedures. They believe it is their right as parents to decide what is best for their children.

A Tested Policy

Whether the government should be allowed to require vaccinations has been brought before the

Rachel Magni pursued a religious opt out so her children did not have to be vaccinated and could still attend school.

U.S. Supreme Court several times. At the turn of the twentieth century, some towns in Massachusetts required their residents to be vaccinated against smallpox, but the Reverend Henning Jacobson refused to do so. In the Supreme Court case *Jacobson v. Massachusetts,* Jacobson's lawyers claimed that the requirement violated their client's Fourteenth Amendment right to liberty. However, the Court found that the state had the right to enforce mandatory vaccinations to protect the health of its citizens. The 1905 ruling set the precedent that ensures state laws requiring vaccinations are upheld. It also showed the Court's belief that in this scenario, public health trumped individual choice. However, the Supreme Court did not uphold mandatory vaccinations in schools until the 1922 ruling in *Zucht v. King*. Since then, states have had the right to enforce mandatory vaccination laws despite the objections of some parents.

In a CDC report on mandatory vaccinations, Kevin Malone and Alan Hinman, attorneys who work with vaccine law, stated the policy has been imperative for preventing the spread of illness. They wrote,

> School vaccination requirements have been a key factor in the prevention and control of vaccine–preventable diseases in the United States. . . . With the increasing numbers of vaccines being introduced and the generally low level of visible threat from disease, continued challenges to school vaccination requirements are expected. School vaccination laws continue to play a central role . . . by preventing disease through high vaccination coverage.[1]

REASONS TO OPT OUT

Parents may opt out of the mandatory vaccination requirements for their children for medical, religious, or philosophical reasons, depending on the state. Typically, parents must submit a signed waiver or a written statement of their objections.

Every state allows parents to opt out for medical reasons. Some children may have medical conditions that make vaccination unsafe for them. In those cases, they are allowed to forgo vaccines.

Other children may live in families whose religious beliefs forbid vaccination. Some religions have restrictions on certain foods. For example, Muslims are not allowed to eat pork. If a vaccine contains products from pigs, they may reject it on religious grounds. All states except for West Virginia and Mississippi accept religious objections to vaccination.

Philosophical Objections

Eighteen states accept philosophical objections. In other words, if parents oppose vaccination for personal, moral, or philosophical reasons, they are not forced to take their children for shots. Parents who oppose vaccination and do not live

The Impact of Exemptions

In a society where almost all people are vaccinated, a single person who refuses vaccination is not at a greatly increased risk. They may be considered safe from infection because the disease is not likely to spread among those around them. However, when too many people opt out of vaccines, the safety of unvaccinated people is greatly reduced. The number of carriers of infectious diseases grows, which puts the community's health at risk.

*Sabrina Rahim, right, opted out of vaccinations for
her children for religious reasons.*

in one of these 18 states may feel strongly enough to
keep their kids out of school. In that case, they end
up homeschooling their children, as did Debra and
Curtis Barnes of Mississippi.

Most parents who oppose vaccines for
philosophical reasons question the necessity and
safety of shots. These parents want to keep toxins
and germs out of their children's bodies. They
are skeptical of vaccine safety statistics and drug
companies that manufacture vaccines and profit

from the sales. They point out that vaccines are not formulated to match each individual's needs. They object that there is no way of knowing if a vaccine will have adverse effects on a child until it is too late. Though doctors and health officials continue to assure parents that the benefits of vaccines far outweigh the risks, some parents believe that any risk is too great.

These parents worry that vaccines may become contaminated, though this happens only in very rare cases. There have also been cases when the live virus in the vaccine was not altered correctly. If this happens, the vaccine can cause disease.

States That Allow Philosophical Objections

Eighteen states allow parents to opt out of vaccines because of personal beliefs. These states include: Arizona, Arkansas, California, Colorado, Idaho, Louisiana, Maine, Michigan, Minnesota, New Mexico, North Dakota, Ohio, Oklahoma, Texas, Utah, Vermont, Washington, and Wisconsin.

In addition, parents point out that the long-term effects of modern vaccines are not fully known. Autoimmune reactions, depressed immune systems, and injured nervous systems might be three long-term consequences of vaccines. These reactions involve the immune and nervous systems not responding or functioning properly, which can cause permanent damage to the body or even death. Other chronic illnesses that have begun to plague children in recent years, including asthma, diabetes, and attention deficit disorders, are sometimes suspected of being linked to vaccines. However, no scientific proof connecting shots to such diseases had been found as of 2010. The causes of these illnesses are difficult to pinpoint and could come from any number of sources. Also, because the majority of children receive vaccines, it is very difficult to know if any long-term effects are related to vaccines, as there is no basis for comparison.

In addition to safety concerns, parents may object to mandatory vaccination because they believe it infringes on their rights. Some parents do not oppose vaccination itself but the fact

Informed Consent

Opponents of mandatory vaccination who cannot opt out believe that the practice denies not only the individual's right to make his or her own medical decisions, but that it also defies informed consent laws. Such laws require doctors to inform, or give patients information on the procedure and make sure that they understand the risks involved. The patients or their legal guardians then must grant their consent, or permission, to go forward.

In opponents' views, mandatory vaccination policies deny them the right to consent. They also feel that vaccine recipients are not adequately informed. Because vaccines are routine procedures in the United States and are considered to be very safe, doctors do not typically discuss the benefits and risks at length. However, materials published by the CDC must be made available to patients before they receive a vaccination.

that it is mandatory. They say that it is their right as parents to choose what is best for their children. Barbara Loe Fisher, cofounder and president of the National Vaccine Information Center, said,

> *If we cannot be free to make informed, voluntary decisions about which pharmaceutical products we are willing to risk our lives for, then we are not free in any sense of the word.*[2]

Health officials worry that those who oppose vaccines are not receiving accurate information.

Conscientious Objectors

In modern times, conscientious objectors are people whose personal beliefs prevent them from fighting in a war. However, the phrase originally applied to people who opposed vaccines. In the late nineteenth century, people who opposed England's widespread vaccine campaign against smallpox called themselves conscientious objectors.

Many people who oppose vaccines rely heavily on popular media, the Internet, and celebrities for information about vaccines. This information is often inaccurate, misleading, or incomplete. Health officials recommend that parents who are thinking about not vaccinating their children speak with their doctors about their concerns.

The stakes are too high to lightly dismiss vaccination, health officials warn. They worry that if too many people reject vaccines, new outbreaks of old diseases may occur.

*Robin Stavola, right, holds a picture of her daughter, who died
at age five due to complications from vaccination.*

Health officials believed a few unvaccinated children led to a 2003 whooping cough outbreak in New York.

NEW OUTBREAKS
OF OLD DISEASES

Many people in the United States have never seen polio, measles, tetanus, and whooping cough, and so they may not fully realize the dangers of these once-common diseases. But medical professionals such as David Keller, former chief of the Infectious Disease and Epidemiology Program with the New Mexico Department of Health, are aware of the tragedies these diseases have brought. He said,

> *I have seen, for example, children with brain injury resulting from not being able to breathe during spells of whooping cough (pertussis). I have seen children and adults unable to walk or even speak their names because of severe brain damage resulting from Haemophilus influenzae type b (Hib) meningitis. . . . I have seen scores of African children and adults crawling on their knees or hobbling with the help of a stick after having polio as youngsters. Finally, I have heard my grandmother's grief after losing her four-year-old daughter to diphtheria. . . . These are heart-rending scenarios, now preventable.[1]*

Keller recognizes the difficulty in deciding to have a child vaccinated, but he argues that these diseases cause far more harm to people than vaccines do. When people go unvaccinated, disease is allowed to spread more easily, and with often-tragic results.

WHOOPING COUGH OUTBREAK

In 2003, a whooping cough outbreak spread through Westchester County, New York. Whooping

cough had become uncommon in developed
countries after the introduction of a vaccine in the
1940s. So why did 19 people become infected during
August and September of 2003?

The outbreak had public health officials worried.
Whooping cough is highly contagious, and mild cases can often be misdiagnosed, especially in adults. Without proper diagnosis and treatment, the disease can spread. It can also be fatal in infants, who are too young to receive the vaccination.

County health officials identified unvaccinated children as the source of the outbreak. Four of

The Threat of Meningitis

In 2005, 18-year-old Ashley Lee, a fresh-man at Indiana University in Bloomington, was diagnosed with meningitis. Lee recovered, but not before doctors had to amputate her left foot. Lee had been unable to get the meningitis vaccine when she visited her doctor before the school year, but she had not been too concerned. Many students who do not receive the vaccine are unaware of the severe conse-quences of a meningitis infection.

Caused by either a viral or bacterial patho-gen, meningitis affects the membranes that protect the brain and spinal cord. Many people recover from the disease, but it can result in deafness, blindness, paralysis, and weak muscles. Amputation may be necessary if the disease prevents blood circulation to limbs and tissue dies. In severe cases, it can cause brain damage and even death. Meningitis can spread quickly where large groups of people gather, such as a day care or a dormitory. For this reason, many schools, colleges, and universi-ties recommend that students get vaccinated against the disease. Many states require college students to receive the vaccine or sign a waiver stating they have read about the disease.

the children infected with the disease had not received the vaccination because of parental choice. Others were either too young to receive the vaccination or had not yet received all of the necessary booster shots. Joshua Lipsman, doctor and Westchester County health commissioner, noted,

> *Certainly one of the take-home lessons here is that children should receive immunizations against vaccine-preventable disease, or we run the risk of outbreaks of those diseases and all the consequent costs in human suffering.* [2]

As Lipsman pointed out, one of the consequences of the decline in vaccinations is an increase in vaccine-preventable infections. When people decline immunization from diseases such as measles, mumps, and whooping cough, they are more likely to become infected, and these diseases can be deadly. Betty Bumpers and Rosalynn Carter are cofounders of Every Child by Two, an organization that promotes early vaccination

How Disease Spreads

Diseases that spread from person to person are called communicable diseases. They can be spread through close contact with an infected person, including sexual contact, and through coughs and sneezes.

Animals and insects such as fleas, mosquitoes, and ticks can spread some diseases to people. For example, mosquitoes can carry malaria, fleas have been known to carry plague, and ticks can carry Lyme disease. Also, mammals infected with rabies can infect people through a bite or a scratch. Some diseases can also be spread by consuming contaminated food and water.

Risk Still Exists

Smallpox is the only disease that has been eradicated worldwide. This was accomplished through a global immunization effort. Although many other diseases are well controlled by vaccines, they still exist. Diseases that are rare in the United States are still causing destruction in other parts of the world, especially in developing nations. Until vaccine-preventable diseases are eradicated in all parts of the world, people who are not immunized are at risk.

of children. They warned, "Make no mistake: The consequences of ignoring safe and effective immunizations are real and can be lethal."[3]

MEASLES OUTBREAKS

The ongoing transmission of endemic measles, or the measles strain native to the United States, was declared eliminated in 2000. However, measles remains common in many developing countries. More than 20 million measles cases occur worldwide each year.

When unvaccinated travelers return to the United States from abroad, they may be unknowingly carrying the measles virus. The pathogen can then spread to people who are either not fully protected or not protected at all. And the disease can spread rapidly, especially in communities where a large number of people are not vaccinated.

Measles is mild in many individuals, who experience high fever, runny nose, coughing, and a rash. However, as many as one in five individuals with measles suffers from more severe symptoms, including diarrhea, ear infection, pneumonia, and brain damage, which can result in death.

In February 2008, a measles outbreak developed in San Diego, California. It began with a child who became ill with measles shortly after returning to the United States from Switzerland. Before the child was diagnosed, at least 11 other children had become infected with the disease. All of the children who fell ill had not been vaccinated.

The CDC reported 131 measles cases in the United States between January and July 2008—the greatest number of measles cases to develop in the country in more than ten years. Fifteen of these patients were hospitalized. More than 90 percent of those infected had not been vaccinated or their vaccination status was unknown. Manny Alvarez, doctor and managing editor of health at *FOXNews.com*, said, "If this continues, we will see outbreaks throughout the entire developed world—something we have never seen before."[4]

Polio in Nigeria

In Africa and the Middle East, polio has become a serious threat to children. The disease most often affects children under age five. It has no cure, and it leaves many children paralyzed. As of 2009, a polio outbreak in Nigeria had reached epidemic proportions. More than half of the world's polio infections develop in that African country, where open sewers and the low rate of vaccinations contribute to the spread of the disease. Because many Muslims in the country are skeptical of Western medicine, they often refuse the vaccine.

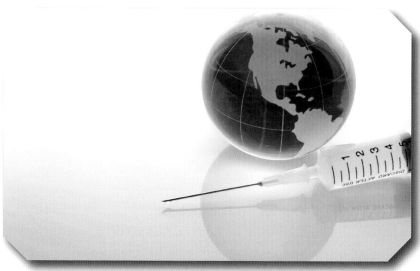

Travelers who are unvaccinated may unknowingly bring a contagious disease with them when they return home.

A measles outbreak also hit Pittsburgh, Pennsylvania, in March 2009. The source of the outbreak was likely a visitor from India. Although vaccination rates in the Pittsburgh area are high, at least five children were confirmed as being infected with the measles virus. More measles outbreaks in other states could signal that the disease is making a comeback. With fewer children being vaccinated against the disease, some health officials worry that it is only a matter of time before scores of children suffer from brain damage or die because of measles. According to the CDC, if everyone worldwide stopped being vaccinated against measles, an estimated 2.7 million deaths would result.

Diagnosis Can Be Difficult

Because vaccine-preventable diseases are so rare, many doctors have never seen them firsthand. Medical professionals may have trouble diagnosing diseases such as diphtheria, tetanus, or measles. Randy Bergen, a pediatrician who specializes in infectious disease, said,

> *Unfortunately, vaccines have been so successful in reducing diseases that not only are parents unaware of the potential severity of these diseases, but many pediatricians have rarely seen them and don't know the potential severity of these diseases either.*[5]

Shelia Creighton's case is an unfortunate example of this. In 2002 she fell in her garden and cut her face. Creighton was treated for the wound in a local hospital. Later, she began to suffer from a stiff neck and had difficulty moving her jaw. She returned to the hospital, but her doctors failed to diagnose her with tetanus. Most of them had never seen a tetanus case before. Shelia Creighton died just four weeks after the initial infection.

In a report to the CDC, Dr. Edward A. Mortimer said that he sees this problem in another area as well: "The diagnosis of diphtheria in the United States is rapidly becoming a lost skill because of the infrequency of the disease in recent years."[6]

In their early stages, many vaccine-preventable diseases display symptoms that could be mistaken for other medical problems. For example, the stiffness and jerky movements of a person suffering from a tetanus infection could be mistaken for seizures. The symptoms could also resemble signs of drug overdose to doctors who are unfamiliar with tetanus. If the proper methods are not used for treating the infection, it can be fatal.

Physicians warn against relying on treatment for vaccine-preventable diseases, which often relies on prompt diagnosis. But even with immediate treatment, many of these illnesses are aggressive. A person's survival is not guaranteed. The best way to protect against such diseases, doctors say, is through vaccination.

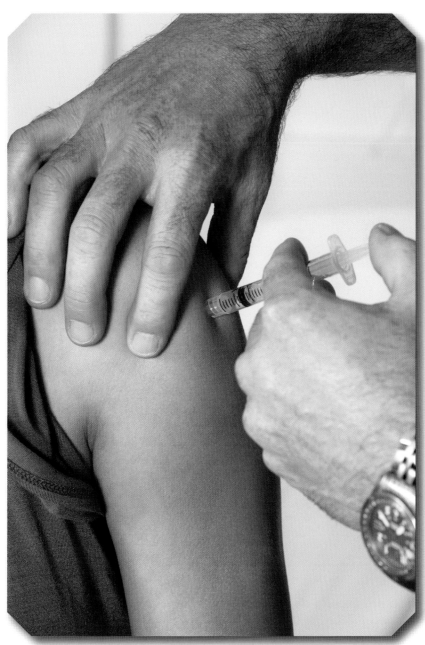

*Doctors recommend vaccination as the best way
to prevent infectious diseases.*

In April 2009, bus passengers in Mexico City, Mexico, wore surgical masks to protect themselves from contracting H1N1.

GLOBAL HEALTH AND VACCINATION

*I*n March 2009, health officials detected a new strain of influenza that was spreading in Mexico. The virus is a strain of type A influenza, subtype H1N1. The virus left numerous people hospitalized, and several died.

By April, H1N1 had spread to the United States. On April 26, 2009, the U.S. government declared a public health emergency. A few days later, WHO assistant director general Keiji Fukuda warned, "It is clear that the virus is spreading and we don't see evidence of it slowing down."[1] Health officials in Europe warned their citizens against unnecessary travel to the United States, but the disease continued to spread. By May 29, 2009, 97 people worldwide had died from the illness. The virus was confirmed to have spread to Australia, Chile, Japan, Panama, Spain, and the United Kingdom. On June 11, WHO raised the H1N1 alert to its highest level, marking the first time an illness had reached this level in 41 years. WHO director general Margaret Chan stated, "We are at the earliest days of a global pandemic."[2]

In the past, influenza pandemics have occurred when a new strain of influenza developed from the type A influenza virus, as H1N1 did. For example, Spanish influenza reached pandemic levels in 1918 and 1919, killing approximately 50 million people worldwide. But it remains to be seen how widespread or deadly the H1N1 virus will become.

Public health officials believe that vaccination is the best strategy to fight the H1N1 virus. After the emergence of H1N1, scientists began investigating a vaccine for the illness. Work on the vaccine did not start until May 2009, two months after the virus first emerged. Approximately five to six months were needed to develop an H1N1 vaccine. In September 2009, the CDC announced an H1N1 vaccine was developed and in the late stages of testing. The organization said shots would be available for the public in fall 2009. The vaccine became available that October.

Influenza Vaccines

A vaccine to prevent seasonal influenza is usually prepared before an outbreak occurs. Each year, different strains of influenza become more dominant. For that reason, the vaccine from one year will not be effective the next year. The influenza vaccine must be reformulated each year. Health specialists meet to decide which strains are most likely to affect a certain area. The decision must be made months in advance to give vaccine manufacturers enough time to make the more than 100 million doses of influenza vaccine needed for the year.

Influenza is an infectious disease that is highly contagious. Symptoms include fever, chills, headache, muscle aches, and weakness. Healthy people may experience only mild symptoms and recover after about a week. But young children, the elderly, and people who already suffer from certain health conditions may be at risk if they are infected. Each year in the United States, between 5 and 20 percent of the population gets infected, about 200,000 people are hospitalized, and about 36,000 people die from influenza.

Researchers are working on developing a universal influenza vaccine. Such a vaccine would protect against all strains and it would not have to be reformulated each year. As of 2010, more testing was still needed.

Emerging Diseases

The H1N1 outbreak of 2009 is one example of an emerging disease—one that has recently been identified or has appeared in a new population. Emerging diseases may be the result of evolution in the organism that causes a disease. Emerging diseases are cause for concern, as modern medicine is not always prepared to fight these new infections. In addition, new diseases are better at resisting the drugs used to treat and prevent illness. According to Professor Mark Woolhouse, an epidemiologist at the University of Edinburgh, Scotland,

> *Pathogens are evolving ways to combat our control methods. The picture is changing and looks as if it will continue to. [Medical professionals are] going to have to run as fast as we can to stay in the same place.*[3]

Furthermore, new diseases are appearing more frequently than they once did. Since 2000, emerging diseases such as West Nile virus, severe acute respiratory syndrome (SARS), avian influenza, and H1N1 have infected thousands of people and caused a number of deaths worldwide.

Because emerging diseases are so difficult to treat and can spread so quickly, the medical community

Director General Margaret Chan of WHO spoke to the United Nations about H1N1 in May 2009.

agrees that vaccination is the most effective method to fight epidemics. As of 2010, the FDA had not approved vaccines that prevent West Nile virus or SARS. A vaccine is available for avian flu, although it is not available for the general public. The U.S. government has purchased a stockpile of the vaccine in the event of a pandemic.

DEVELOPING NATIONS

In developing nations, infectious diseases, including vaccine-preventable diseases, are a major problem. Every year, between 14 million and 17 million people, most of whom live in developing nations, die because of infectious diseases. Children are especially vulnerable. Malaria, dengue, tuberculosis, cholera, and yellow fever reach epidemic proportions, especially in South America and Africa. In the first half of 2009, a meningitis epidemic in Nigeria had resulted in more than 2,000 deaths. The country also battles a polio epidemic, as does India. Outbreaks of polio have spread to other parts of Africa and Asia.

Organizations such as WHO work toward preventing the spread of these diseases. They focus on improving health systems so that more people have access to vaccination and

Yellow Fever Vaccine

Yellow fever regularly occurs in 33 African countries. Approximately 200,000 people contract yellow fever each year, and 30,000 of those people die from the disease. In order to prevent yellow fever epidemics, WHO recommends yellow fever vaccinations to coincide with children's measles immunization. However, as of 2000, only 15 African countries had implemented the recommendation.

treatment. Keeping track of outbreaks allows the groups to quickly send in medical personnel to affected areas. Rapid response can go a long way toward controlling disease.

Infectious diseases can spread easily from developing nations to the rest of the world. With increased globalization and the ease of worldwide travel, these diseases can reach across the globe in a matter of days or weeks. Within the close quarters of an airplane, illness spreads easily among passengers. Once infected passengers reach their destinations, they are likely to spread the illness to others. Often, a disease can reach epidemic proportions before action can be taken to control its spread.

To prevent the spread of infectious diseases around the world, WHO recommends travelers stay up-to-date on vaccinations, especially those needed for foreign travel. The organization states vaccination is the best way for individuals to avoid developing disease. Vaccination also decreases the chance of travelers spreading the disease to others.

Bioterrorism

After the terrorist attacks in New York City and Washington DC on September 11, 2001, government officials became concerned about the potential for bioterrorism. This method of attack involves releasing harmful bacteria, viruses, or poisons in order to cause severe illness in a population. These disease-causing materials could potentially be used to contaminate food or water supplies.

In 2001, a small number of people received powdered anthrax in the mail. Anthrax is a bacterial infectious disease that chiefly affects the skin and lungs. Symptoms of the disease include fever, vomiting, and stomach pain. Death can occur if treatment is not rapidly received. The 2001 anthrax attack killed five people.

Government officials fear anthrax could be used for bioterrorism. While an anthrax vaccine does exist, it is not routinely administered to everyone. Only people who have a high risk of contracting the disease—those in the military and certain other professions—currently receive the vaccine.

Likely Attack

In 2008, a Department of Homeland Security report predicted that terrorists would attempt a biological attack within the next five years. It said, "Officials are concerned about the possibility of infections to thousands of U.S. citizens, overwhelming regional health care systems."[4]

Why Was the Smallpox Virus Not Destroyed?

When WHO declared smallpox to be eradicated in 1980, the organization recommended that smallpox vaccination end worldwide. The organization also recommended that two samples of the virus be kept—one at a CDC laboratory in Atlanta, Georgia, and one in Russia.

Smallpox was arguably one of the most destructive infectious diseases in history, and government and health officials believe that it could be one of the main diseases used in biological warfare. Why, then, was the virus not destroyed? One reason it has been kept is in case the virus is needed for future research purposes. But some people have protested that terrorist groups or nations could obtain the virus to use in bioterrorism. The question continues to be debated.

Smallpox is another disease that officials worry could be used for bioterrorism. Because smallpox has been eradicated, the vaccine is no longer administered to the general public. Only two laboratories in the world, one in the United States and one in Russia, hold samples of the smallpox virus. These samples are highly guarded and would be difficult for terrorists to obtain. However, the stakes are high. Some scientists warn that an attack using smallpox could kill millions of people. A number of top U.S. government officials were vaccinated for smallpox starting in 2001. Once more of the vaccine became available, it was offered to health-care workers and soldiers. Someday, the vaccine may once again be made available to the general public.

Emergency response to a biological attack is a major area of concern. In the event of such an attack, many people would be infected at once, especially those who had not been vaccinated. If anthrax or smallpox were used, this would mean a great number of people. The infected would likely overwhelm hospitals and other health-care facilities. In such a scenario, many would die from lack of proper treatment. Government and health organizations have response plans in place in the event of a bioterrorist attack. As of 2010, smallpox and anthrax vaccinations were not recommended for the general public, but if an attack were to occur, those vaccines would be put into effect.

Another challenge for emergency responders would be a lack of vaccines. Government leaders and public health authorities are focusing on smallpox and anthrax as the most likely substances that could be used in a bioterrorism attack. However, other possible agents, including Ebola and tuberculosis, are numerous. No vaccines exist for some of the agents. But, even in cases where vaccines do exist, problems abound. Because it is difficult to anticipate which agent might be used in an attack, manufacturers have not made enough doses to protect everyone in the event of an emergency. They would not be able to produce and distribute the large

number of doses the public would require. For the same reason, a vaccination program to protect the public against such a variety of diseases would be impractical. ⌐

In the event of a bioterrorist attack, many people
might be infected at once.

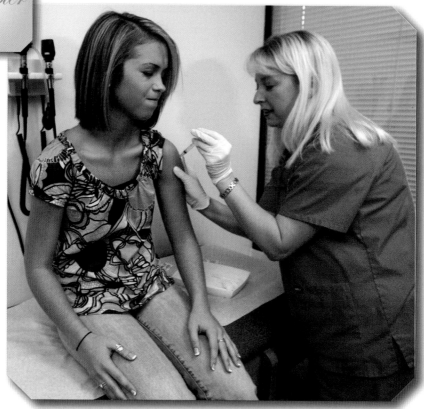

Lauren Fant receives the third and final shot for the HPV vaccine.

THE FUTURE OF VACCINES

Researchers are continually working on developing new vaccines and improving existing ones. As more effective vaccines become available, doctors believe both vaccine safety and public health will improve.

In 2006, the FDA approved the use of the human papillomavirus (HPV) vaccine in the United States. HPV is a sexually transmitted disease that is responsible for 90 percent of cases of genital warts and 70 percent of cases of cervical cancer. It is also the most common sexually transmitted disease.

The HPV vaccine is only the second vaccine that was developed to help prevent cancer. (The first was for hepatitis B, which can cause liver cancer.) The FDA has approved the HPV vaccine for females and males ages 9 to 26. Although the vaccine has received a good deal of attention, some women have identified barriers to receiving it, including its high cost, the inconvenience of receiving the three injections necessary, and poor knowledge about HPV and its connection to cervical cancer.

Other vaccines are in development. For example, one researcher in Ohio and another in Louisiana are studying a vaccine strategy against ear infections. Ear infections are the most frequently diagnosed illness in children under the age of 15 in the United States. The vaccine could be applied in drop form, placed onto the child's ear and then rubbed in, so no needles would be used. The vaccine would protect against this common ailment, but it could also lead to prevention of other diseases, such as respiratory illnesses.

The Search for a Malaria Vaccine

Malaria is a devastating disease transmitted to people by mosquitoes. Infected individuals develop high fevers and flulike symptoms. If left untreated, malaria patients can become severely ill and die. Each year, between 350 million and 500 million people worldwide develop malaria and more than one million die from it. Malaria is especially prevalent in Africa, where treatment is out of reach for many who need it. There, it kills one in 20 children under the age of five.

Researchers have been trying to develop a malaria vaccine for more than 70 years but have been unsuccessful. As of 2007, approximately 70 experimental vaccines existed worldwide, but none

Cancer Vaccines

Researchers are working to develop vaccines to prevent cancer in healthy people. Though many different types of cancer can affect various parts of the body, they are most often identified by abnormal or uncontrolled cell division, which results in tumors.

Vaccines exist for two cancer-causing viruses: hepatitis B, which can cause liver cancer, and human papillomavirus (HPV), which can cause cervical cancer. Other cancers caused by viruses may one day be preventable through vaccines.

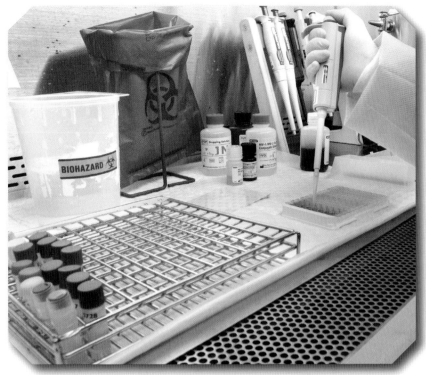

A lab technician tests the blood of participants in the Thai HIV vaccine study.

have been approved for general use. Most health experts in the field do not think a malaria vaccine will be developed for several years.

AN AIDS VACCINE

A vaccine to prevent human immunodeficiency virus (HIV) and acquired immunodeficiency syndrome (AIDS) is also needed and has been researched for years. HIV is the virus that leads to AIDS. Although HIV can be effectively managed for years, no known cure exists. In 2007, it was estimated that 33.2 million people worldwide were living with HIV. More than two-thirds of the affected were living in sub-Saharan Africa. Each year, approximately 2.7 million people are newly infected with HIV. Worldwide, a total of 2 million people died from AIDS in 2007.

An effective vaccine against the HIV virus would go a long way in the battle against AIDS, but the virus is difficult to fight. There are nine types of HIV. Any vaccine would prevent infection only against one of those types. In addition, once a person is infected, the virus quickly begins to mutate, or change.

Rather than work on a vaccine to prevent infection of HIV, some researchers are working on vaccines that would affect T-cells. These cells are a type of white blood cells that are important to the immune system. Specifically, T-cells contribute to the body's ability to respond to new pathogens that enter the body. HIV destroys T-cells, leaving an infected person less capable of fighting off illness.

As a result of this type of AIDS vaccine, T-cells would destroy other cells infected with HIV. This kind of vaccine would not be able to prevent HIV infection, but it would decrease the amount of HIV in a person's body and, researchers hope, prevent the development of AIDS.

In September 2009, it was reported that, for the first time, an HIV vaccine protected a small percentage of human study participants from contracting the virus. Dr. Anthony S. Fauci, director of the National Institute of Allergy and Infectious Diseases, said of the vaccine, "I don't want to use a word like 'breakthrough,' but I don't think there's any doubt that this is a very important result."[1]

But almost immediately,

Vaccine Shortages

Sometimes more vaccine is needed than manufacturers can provide. This causes vaccine shortages, which can last from a few weeks to several months. Shortages often happen with the influenza vaccine and have also occurred with tetanus shots.

Many factors can cause shortages. Perhaps a drug company cannot manufacture enough of the vaccine or must stop making it because of internal production problems. Sometimes batches are contaminated and must be destroyed. Some vaccine manufacturers may leave the market, placing the large amount of vaccine production on fewer companies. Or there is simply a delay in transporting the vaccines.

During a shortage, many people must wait for their shots. Priority for receiving the vaccines will often go to the elderly, those with weak immune systems, or medical professionals who are often exposed to pathogens. When shortages have interfered with children's vaccination schedules, health officials have released alternate guidelines for parents to follow.

a debate emerged regarding the vaccine's partial effectiveness, with some scientists questioning if the results were coincidental. Still, the vaccine may help guide future research. Its full impact remains to be seen.

COMBATING DISEASE

The medical community generally agrees that vaccines have proven to be the most effective way to prevent the spread of many devastating illnesses that once plagued society. On rare occasions, however, vaccines have caused harm. The debate surrounding vaccination continues: Do the benefits of vaccines outweigh the risks? And if they do, should vaccines be mandatory? In what cases should society allow exemptions for those who oppose vaccination? What is more important—individual rights or the public's health? Is more research needed into the link

HPV Vaccine Opposition

The HPV vaccine is recommended for females and males ages 9 to 26. However, because it targets a sexually transmitted disease, the vaccine has been controversial. Some parents feel the vaccine would force them into a conversation with their children about sex. Other parents fear that by allowing the vaccine, they would inadvertently be granting their approval for premarital sex. Some oppose the vaccine's high cost. Each of the three shots costs $120, making the complete vaccine $360 total. Still, medical professionals say the vaccine is the best method currently available to protect against HPV and cervical cancer.

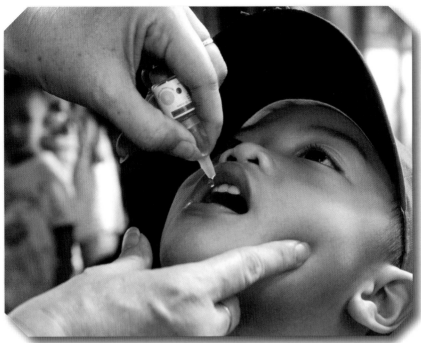

An Indonesian child received the oral vaccine for polio in 2006.

between vaccination and autism? How can the scientific community and the government make sure that vaccines are safe and effective 100 percent of the time?

While communities in the United States wrestle with such questions, international public health officials worry about the lack of vaccines worldwide. The questions they face include: How can we develop vaccines more quickly to combat emerging diseases?

How can we better make those available to people in developing countries?

In either case, the questions are not easily answered. ⌐

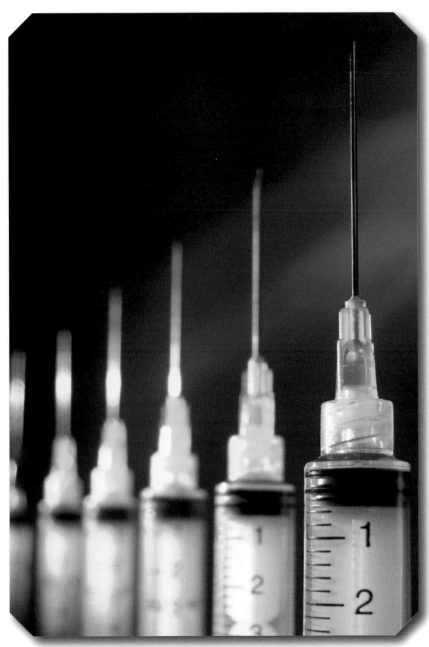

Vaccination has had both successes and failures and contributes to the debate of public health versus individual choice.

TIMELINE

10,000 BCE

Smallpox likely
develops in Africa.

900s CE

Chinese healers
develop the process
of variolation to
induce immunity
to smallpox.

1721

Lady Mary Wortley
Montagu introduces
variolation to
England.

1955

Jonas Salk's polio
vaccine is approved
for use in the
United States.

1960

Dr. Bernice Eddy
discovers that
polio vaccines
contain cancer-
causing agents, but
her findings are
suppressed.

1963

Measles vaccine is
used for the first time.

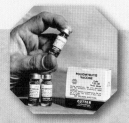

Late 1700s

The smallpox vaccine is developed in the late eighteenth century.

1801

More than 100,000 people have been vaccinated with smallpox vaccine.

1929

A contaminated tuberculosis vaccine kills 72 children in Lübeck, Germany.

1980

The World Health Organization declares smallpox to be eradicated.

1988

Congress creates the National Vaccine Injury Compensation Program in order to compensate those harmed by vaccines.

1994

The Immunization Action Coalition is launched to increase immunization rates and prevent the spread of illness.

TIMELINE

1998

Andrew Wakefield publishes a study indicating that vaccines may cause autism in some children. It is later discredited.

2001

Because of the threat of bioterrorism, high-ranking government officials are vaccinated for smallpox.

2001

Thimerosal is removed or reduced in vaccines in the United States.

2008

The National Vaccine Injury Compensation Program awards compensation to Hannah Poling, a girl with autism.

2008

A total of 131 measles cases are reported in the United States between January and July.

2009

In February, a court rules that there is no proven link between vaccines and autism.

2006	2007	2007
The FDA approves an HPV vaccine.	Two million people worldwide die from AIDS.	Approximately 70 experimental malaria vaccines exist.

2009	2009	2009
In April, a new strain of influenza, H1N1, is declared a pandemic.	In September, an HIV vaccine shows partial success in preventing recipients from contracting the virus.	In October, a vaccine for H1N1 is released.

ESSENTIAL FACTS

AT ISSUE

Opposed

❖ Vaccines are not always effective at preventing disease.

❖ The long-term effects of vaccines are unknown. They may potentially cause asthma, attention deficit disorder, diabetes, and autism.

❖ Contaminated vaccines or vaccines that are not completely neutralized have caused severe illness, and sometimes death.

❖ Mandatory vaccination impedes parents' rights to decide what is best for their children.

In Favor

❖ Vaccines have drastically decreased the incidence of many diseases and eradicated smallpox.

❖ Vaccination protects the public from disease by limiting the number of people who can become infected and spread illness.

❖ Decreased vaccination has caused outbreaks of once-preventable diseases.

❖ There is no proven link between vaccination and autism.

CRITICAL DATES

1801
More than 100,000 people had been vaccinated with Edward Jenner's smallpox vaccine.

1948
The World Health Organization was founded to create better health systems around the world and improve global health.

1988
The National Vaccine Injury Compensation Program was created in the United States in order to compensate those harmed by vaccines.

2001
In response to concerns about the safety of vaccines, the United States required that thimerosal be removed or reduced in vaccines.

2009
A special U.S. court ruled that there is no proven link between vaccines and autism.

QUOTES
"Public health means recognizing that complete personal responsibility is unattainable. Within limits, we must all help look after one another—that is our social contract." —*Arthur Allen,* Vaccine: The Controversial Story of Medicine's Greatest Lifesaver

"If you want to vaccinate your children, go ahead. But don't force me to vaccinate my children. These children are entrusted to us." —*Debra Barnes, president of the Jackson chapter of the Mississippi Vaccination Information Center*

ADDITIONAL RESOURCES

SELECT BIBLIOGRAPHY

Allen, Arthur. *Vaccine: The Controversial Story of Medicine's Greatest Lifesaver.* New York, NY: W.W. Norton, 2007.

Link, Kurt. *The Vaccine Controversy: The History, Use, and Safety of Vaccinations.* Westport, CT: Praeger Publishers, 2005.

Miller, Neil Z. *Vaccines: Are They Really Safe and Effective?* Santa Fe, NM: New Atlantean Press, 2002.

Neustaedter, Randall. *The Vaccine Guide: Risks and Benefits for Children and Adults.* Berkeley, CA: North Atlantic Books, 2002.

FURTHER READING

Barnard, Bryn. *Outbreak: Plagues That Changed History.* New York, NY: Crown, 2005.

Farrell, Jeanette. *Invisible Enemies: Stories of Infectious Disease.* New York, NY: Farrar, Straus, and Giroux, 2005.

Phalan, Glen. *Killing Germs, Saving Lives: The Quest for the First Vaccines.* Washington DC: National Geographic, 2006.

WEB LINKS

To learn more about the vaccination debate, visit ABDO Publishing Company online at **www.abdopublishing.com.** Web sites about the vaccination debate are featured on our Book Links page. These links are routinely monitored and updated to provide the most current information available.

For More Information

For more information on this subject, contact or visit the following organizations:

Centers for Disease Control and Prevention
1600 Clifton Road, Atlanta, GA 30333
800-232-4636
www.cdc.gov
The Centers for Disease Control and Prevention is a government organization that works to monitor and prevent disease and to inform the public about health.

Immunization Action Coalition
1573 Selby Avenue, Suite 234, St. Paul, MN 55104
651-647-9009
www.immunize.org
The Immunization Action Coalition works to improve the effectiveness of vaccination, to increase the number of people being vaccinated, and to provide the public with vaccination-related information.

Institute for Vaccine Safety
Johns Hopkins Bloomberg School of Public Health
615 N. Wolfe Street, Room W5041, Baltimore, MD 21205
www.vaccinesafety.edu
The Institute for Vaccine Safety provides objective information on the safety and effectiveness of vaccinations.

National Vaccine Information Center
407 Church Street, Suite H, Vienna, VA 22180
703-938-0342
www.nvic.org
The National Vaccine Information Center works toward increased vaccine safety and the implementation of informed consent laws.

GLOSSARY

antibody
A protein in the body that responds when something foreign, such as a virus, enters the body; an antibody fights infection and protects against future disease.

bacteria
Common single-celled organisms; some have the ability to cause disease.

bioterrorism
A terrorist attack that uses chemicals or disease-causing material to spread illness in a population.

communicable disease
An illness that can be spread from person to person.

endemic
Something, such as a disease, that occurs in a specific area.

epidemic
Widespread occurrence of a disease.

eradicate
To end or do away with something.

globalization
The development of an increasingly integrated worldwide economy.

immune system
The group of organs and cells that allow the body to fight off infection.

immunity
The ability to resist infection.

immunization
> The process of becoming immune to a disease; a vaccination is a kind of immunization.

infectious disease
> An illness that is likely to quickly spread to others.

inoculate
> To vaccinate.

microbe
> A microorganism, including bacteria or fungi.

outbreak
> The sudden increased occurrence of a disease within a small area.

pandemic
> Worldwide spread of disease.

pathogen
> The agent that causes disease, such as bacteria, a virus, or another microbe.

toxin
> A poisonous substance.

vaccine
> A substance used to stimulate an immune system response to a particular disease, providing a person with immunity to the disease.

variolation
> An early form of vaccination created by Chinese healers.

virus
> A microscopic agent that causes disease.

SOURCE NOTES

Chapter 1. Vaccines and Illness

1. Chris Joyner. "Parents Home-school to avoid vaccinating their kids." *USA Today.* 22 Oct. 2008. 18 May 2009 <http://www.usatoday.com/news/health/2008-10-21-home-school-vaccinate_N.htm>.

2. Laurie Tarkan. "Vaccinations Battling Disease; People Battling Vaccines." 28 Mar. 2008. 13 Oct. 2009 <http://health.nytimes.com/ref/health/healthguide/esn-vaccinations-expert.html>.

3. "Parents sound off on childhood vaccine divide." *Msnbc.com.* 24 Aug. 2008. 18 May 2009 <http://www.msnbc.msn.com/id/26334836/>.

4. "Why Get Vaccinated?" *Infectious Disease: Vaccines & Human Immunity.* 2009. Science Museum of the National Academy of Sciences. 18 May 2009 <http://www.koshland-science-museum.org/exhib_infectious/vaccines_01.jsp>.

5. Alice Park. "How Safe Are Vaccines?" *Time.* 21 May 2008. 19 May 2009 <http://www.time.com/time/health/article/0,8599,1808438,00.html>.

6. Jennifer Steinhauer. "Public Health Risk Seen as Parents Reject Vaccines." *New York Times.* 21 Mar. 2008. 15 June 2009 <http://www.nytimes.com/2008/03/21/us/21vaccine.html?_r=1>.

7. Arthur Allen. *Vaccine: The Controversial Story of Medicine's Greatest Lifesaver.* New York, NY: W.W. Norton, 2007. 17.

Chapter 2. What Is Vaccination?

1. "Ten Great Public Health Achievements—United States, 1900-1999." Centers for Disease Control and Prevention. 2 May 2001. 26 Aug. 2009 <http://www.cdc.gov/mmwr/preview/mmwrhtml/00056796.htm>.

2. David Keller. "Are Vaccines Worth It?" 31 Dec. 2001. Immunization Action Coalition. 30 May 2009 <http://www.immunize.org/reports/report042.asp>.

Chapter 3. The Rise of Vaccination

1. Nicolau Barquet and Pere Domingo. "Smallpox: The Triumph over the Most Terrible of the Ministers of Death." *Annals of Internal Medicine* 127.8 (1997): 635. 25 May 2009 <http://www.annals.org/cgi/content/full/127/8_Part_1/635>.

2. Nicolau Barquet and Pere Domingo. "Smallpox: The Triumph over the Most Terrible of the Ministers of Death." *Annals of Internal Medicine* 127.8 (1997): 639. 25 May 2009 <http://www.annals.org/cgi/content/full/127/8_Part_1/635>.

3. Arthur Allen. *Vaccine: The Controversial Story of Medicine's Greatest Lifesaver.* New York, NY: W.W. Norton, 2007. 49–50.

Chapter 4. A History of Vaccine Errors

1. John Rowan Wilson. *Margin of Safety.* New York, NY: Doubleday, 1963. 18.

Chapter 5. Autism and Vaccines

1. Claudia Wallis. "Case Study: Autism and Vaccines." *Time.* 10 Mar. 2008. 1 June 2009 <http://www.time.com/time/health/article/0,8599,1721109,00.html>.

2. Jenny McCarthy and Jim Carrey. "Jenny McCarthy: My Son's Recovery from Autism." *CNN.com.* 4 Apr. 2008. 1 June 2009 <http://www.cnn.com/2008/US/04/02/mccarthy.autismtreatment/index.html>.

3. "Snyder v. Secretary of The Department of Health and Human Services." No. 01-162V. 12 Feb. 2009. 19 July 2009 <ftp://autism.uscfc.uscourts.gov/autism/vaccine/Vowell.Snyder.pdf>.

SOURCE NOTES CONTINUED

Chapter 6. Opposition to Mandatory Vaccination
1. Kevin M. Malone and Alan R. Hinman. "Vaccination Mandates:
The Public Health Imperative and Individual Rights." Centers for
Disease Control and Prevention. 13 July 2009 <http://www.cdc.
gov/vaccines/vac-gen/policies/downloads/vacc_mandates_chptr13.
pdf>.
2. Barbara Loe Fisher. "Vaccine Freedom of Choice." 16 Oct.
2008. National Vaccine Information Center. 7 June 2009
<http://www.nvic.org/informed-consent/freedomofchoice.aspx>.

Chapter 7. New Outbreaks of Old Diseases
1. David Keller. "Are Vaccines Worth It?" 31 Dec. 2001.
Immunization Action Coalition. 30 May 2009 <http://www.
immunize.org/reports/report042.asp>.
2. Richard Pérez-Peña. "Vaccine Refusal Is Cited in Whooping
Cough Cases." *New York Times*. 7 Oct. 2003. 2 June 2009 <http://
www.nytimes.com/2003/10/07/nyregion/vaccine-refusal-is-cited-
in-whooping-cough-cases.html>.
3. Betty Bumpers and Rosalynn Carter. "Unprotected People
#38: Some Parents Fall for Vaccination Scare Stories, with Deadly
Results." 1 Jan. 2001. Immunization Action Coalition. 30 May
2009 <http://www.immunize.org/reports/report038.asp>.
4. "Measles Outbreak Spreads to 15 States, Largest in 10 Years."
FOXNews.com. 10 July 2008. 2 June 2009 <http://www.foxnews.
com/story/0,2933,379388,00.html>.
5. Patti Neighmond. "Is Vaccine Refusal Worth the Risk?" *Morning
Edition*. 26 May 2009. NPR. 7 June 2009 <http://www.npr.org/
templates/story/story.php?storyId=104523437>.
6. "If We Stop Vaccinating…" CDC National Vaccine Program
Office. 7 June 2009 <http://www.hhs.gov/nvpo/part6.htm>.

Chapter 8. Global Health and Vaccination

1. Matthew Price. "Five New UK Flu Cases Confirmed." *BBC News.* 29 Apr. 2009. 5 June 2009 <http://news.bbc.co.uk/2/hi/americas/8024611.stm>.

2. Nick Cumming-Bruce and Andrew Jacobs. "W.H.O. Raises Alert Level As Flu Spreads to 74 Countries." *New York Times.* 11 Jun. 2009. 19 June 2009 <http://www.nytimes.com/2009/06/12/world/12who.html>.

3. Paul Rincon. "'Faster Emergence' for Diseases." *BBC News.* 20 Feb. 2006. 5 June 2009 <http://news.bbc.co.uk/2/hi/science/nature/4732924.stm>.

4. "Bioterrorism Risks and Preparedness." *New York Times.* 9 Jan. 2009. 6 June 2009 <http://topics.blogs.nytimes.com/2009/01/09/bioterrorism-risks-and-preparedness/>.

Chapter 9. The Future of Vaccines

1. Donald G. McNeil Jr. "For First Time, AIDS Vaccine Shows Some Success." *New York Times.* 24 Sep. 2009. 30 Sep. 2009 <http://www.nytimes.com/2009/09/25/health/research/25aids.html?scp=1&sq=aids%20vaccine&st=cse>.

INDEX

About the Author

Jill Sherman is an author and editor living in Philadelphia. Her writing spans such topics as the Hindenburg disaster and alternative fuels. She is the author of several books in the Essential Library series. Jill also enjoys practicing yoga and playing bass guitar.

Photo Credits

Patricia Hofmeester/iStockphoto, cover, 3; Brad Killer/iStockphoto, 6; Red Line Editorial, 9; John Bazemore/AP Images, 17; iStockphoto, 18; AP Images, 21, 43, 44, 96; Evan Vucci/AP Images, 25; Keystone Features/Stringer/Getty Images, 26; Santosh Basak/AP Images, 28, 97 (bottom); North Wind Picture Archives/Photolibrary, 33; North Wind Picture Archives, 34, 37, 97 (top); Steve Parsons/AP Images, 47, 98 (top); Jose Luis Magana/AP Images, 49; Stefan Klein/iStockphoto, 53; Mel Evans/AP Images, 54, 63, 98 (bottom); Lisa Poole/AP Images, 56, 59; Sean Locke/iStockphoto, 64; Günay Mutlu/iStockphoto, 70; Ron Sumners/iStockphoto, 73; Brennan Linsley/AP Images, 74; Laurent Gillieron/AP Images, 78; Katsumi Kasahara/AP Images, 85; John Amis/AP Images, 86; Apichart Weerawong/AP Images, 89, 99; Tatan Syuflana/AP Images, 93; Egor Mopanko/iStockphoto, 95